For Colin :

A MOON AT THE DOOR

with my thanks for the happy
outcome of the submission of
this book to the E.J.P.S.
Hope you enjoy the poems,
Best wishes,

Wanda

November 1998

Also by Wanda Barford

Sweet Wine and Bitter Herbs
(Flambard, 1996)

A MOON AT THE DOOR

Wanda Barford

FLAMBARD

in association with
The European Jewish Publication Society

ACKNOWLEDGEMENTS

Some poems in this collection have previously appeared in:
Acumen, The Dybbuk of Delight, European Judaism,
The Jewish Quarterly, Other Poetry and *Voices, Israel.*

Flambard Press wishes to thank Northern Arts
for its financial support.

Flambard Press also wishes to thank the European
Jewish Publication Society for supporting this publication.

First published in England in 1999 by Flambard Press
Stable Cottage, East Fourstones, Hexham NE47 5DX

Typeset by Barbara Sumner
Cover design by Gainford Design Associates
Printed by Cromwell Press, Trowbridge, Wiltshire

A CIP catalogue record for this book
is available from the British Library

ISBN 1 873226 33 0

CONTENTS

PREFACE

In the middle of this century man walked on the moon. In the title-poem of my collection, the opposite happens: the moon comes to me, it rolls to my door and dazzles me. My mother steps out as if from a carriage. She is 'the woman in the moon' with her round full cheeks, black hair parted in the middle, piercing black eyes, strong classical nose and fine skin.

These poems are about her and about how I perceived her at different stages in my life. Some address her directly in the second person (even when she's no longer there); others describe her more objectively in the third.

Born in Rhodes in 1903 under the Ottoman Crescent (another moon) she retained – as did her father who acted as judge in the Turkish court – a respect and affection for the magnanimous Turks who welcomed into their midst the Jews expelled from Spain in 1492. Her education, however, was French, and French became the language and the literature with which she had a life-long love affair.

In 1912 the Italians invaded the Dodecanese. Had it remained Turkish, the Jews of the islands, all 2000 of them (which included her parents and many members of her extended family), would have been spared deportation to Auschwitz. At the time, the Turkish consul saved many of them by claiming they were nationals of a neutral country.

In 1926, by then married, she and my father had gone to live in Milan. She never felt the same attraction for the language and literature of Italy. Its music, however, cast a spell over her, and by the time Mussolini's racial laws took hold and set us all on the road again, she had become an habitué of La Scala and of the Sala Giuseppe Verdi (where she had previously picked a pianoforte teacher for me).

When World War II broke out in September 1939, we had been in Southern Rhodesia just one month. There, my mother became the quintessential exile, the outsider, and passed on the restless feelings of dislocation, of non-belonging, to me and my brother. Speaking no English, playing no tennis or bridge, and not liking afternoon tea-parties, she suffered until she began to find one or two people of like mind. Had she belonged to a later generation, she would undoubtedly have pursued a university education and a career.

She was sixty before her dream of living and breathing the intellectual life of Paris came true. My father had died in Rhodesia; she packed everything up and arrived in Paris in 1963, to live out the happiest days of her life, barring perhaps her childhood in Rhodes. She died in her flat in Courbevoie alone, no rabbi or doctor in attendance, as had been her ardent wish. She loved and valued solitude. 'Solitude,' she once said, 'is earned.'

All her adult life she kept notebooks (first in English, then in French) in which she wrote poems, thoughts – her own and other people's – and a novel. She only once sent a sheaf of poems (in manuscript) to a Paris publisher who returned it with a very laudatory letter I still have. She would not have had the stamina to paper her wall with rejection slips – she was too proud for that.

On the front page of her novel, I found she had translated some lines of Rabindranath Tagore:

Et la voix de la mère, le soir,
donnait un sens aux étoiles.

She certainly gave meaning to my life, and through these poems I thank her.

WANDA BARFORD
Hampstead, 1998

A MOON AT THE DOOR

I dreamed
a moon drew up
with you inside it

You stepped out young
your cheeks fleshed out
your black hair shining

I stood on the threshold
calling your name over and over
and I died of brightness

TO MARKET

Mother
      Mother
is it far
from your place
to mine?
And are there
stones on the path?

Not a single stone, Child;
it's a smooth
and easy way.

Mother
      Mother
now you're here
help me choose.
Spinach? Should it be
blue-green with wide leaves
and long white stems,
or clusters of small leaves
that cook fast and tender?

Child, I no longer
need to choose;
all choices are yours now,
make them wisely.

So saying,
she goes back,
up the winding path
and out of sight.

LAMENT

after Stevie Smith

Girl from the ghetto
Eyes of a doe
You trouble me so
You trouble me so.

Girl with one foot
On the slimback chair
The chair on the pebbles
And your dark dark hair
In coils and a bun
And your skin of a nun
And your faraway stare
How I wish I'd been there
To see you nineteen
Dreaming your dream.

Girl from the ghetto
Lips like pink roe
Cheeks all aglow
You're ready to go
And find your true love
'Sent from above'
And marry him too
(As was proper to do).

Girl from the ghetto
Eyes of a doe
You've brightened me
Darkened me troubled me
Heartened me so
I cannot let go
Ever let go.

YOU, IN A BOAT

You passed
Under my window
Where the river flows;
You and your favourite son
In a pleasure boat. He,
Spreadeagled over the wooden slats,
Smiled and smiled; you sitting opposite
Hugged yourself tightly.

Your face
Luminous and round
Shone up at me.
And there *was* time
To wave and smile,
For the boat had stopped
A moment at a signal…
Then it was gone.

Under my window
The river flows.

AFTER A VISIT

When I woke, she'd left,
and darkness invaded the room
like the ending of a chapter.

The knowledge she was gone
spread over me like a fever:
it burnt my eyes, my throat, as if
I'd stared too long at the sun.

I fought it with the resources
she had so diligently
taught me to muster.

I've come through
reduced like a dried fruit…
I'm looking for thin affections now,
and for the comforting neutrality
of trees and sky.

JEALOUS

The two of you
on the veranda
sitting on osier chairs,

a criss-cross of chatter
and laughter
as you sip from china cups.

On the dry rose-lawn
I pace
learning lines, but listening.

Excluded, I make
your friend's beautiful face
coarsen.

I would spirit her away
so she leaves you to me –
leaves me the pink house,

the veranda
with the red cement floor,
the wilting petunias,

in the low wall –
all that dry, spiky garden,
and the unreal African you.

'YES, MADAM'

'Fetch your blanket,'
she said to the houseboy,
'and sleep in the kitchen
till the boss comes home.'
'Yes, madam,' he replied.

The Mau Mau
was spoken of
at bridge and tea parties.
Father would be late back
from his Masonic lodge.

Uneasy, she asked the boy:
'If your brothers
in the Freedom Movement
told you to kill me,
you wouldn't do it, would you?'

'Yes, madam,' he replied.

EMPTY

Back from school – usual *Hello Mum* – no answer.
Go to kitchen – everything put away, neat.
Call again – silence deepens, moves from room to room
ahead of me, a ghost beckoning…
Search all downstairs, then up – might be on her bed
resting – no one – is she dead?
Come down again – go out the back
to servants' kaia – 'Where is Madam?'
Tina aikona azi. Start to panic –
How could she do this, and without warning?
Must phone neighbours – first her sister up the road.

Found her.
She's there sipping tea –
comes to the phone: 'Darling,
do I have to be there
every time you come home from school?'

FLORESTAN AND EUSEBIUS

'Schumann,' you said,
'play me some Schumann,
my favourite: *The Merry Peasant*.'
I fumble for the bass line
and can't remember the right-hand chords.

That's in the dream.
Awake, I played it well.
And others, like *First Loss*,
whose tune I sang to my doll
until two pink tears tracked down her cheeks.

But *Papillons* defeated me,
and the *Symphonic Studies*; I couldn't cope
with the savage mood swings:
your joyous Florestan
against my melancholy Eusebius.

So we're back in the dream:
to your shouting from the kitchen,
'practise your left hand,
more scales and arpeggios,
your left hand must ring out.'

AT DAYBREAK

The Colossus sun is punctual as Sarotta, the maid
 who wakes her, the house still asleep.
Each day the same routine: a piercing call with a cup
 of Turkish coffee, to lift her from the deep.

She climbs to the top of the house
 up the out-of-bounds wooden stair
To learn her schoolgirl lines on the terrace – Racine this week –
 in that pellucid air.

The lime-washed terrace turns from moon to pink,
 the sea from black to violet;
The Anatolian coast sheds its heavy cloak
 for a misty-fine pink net.

Ships in the harbour sound their melancholy horns,
 setting out to more important lands.
She waves to them, dreams journeys, laughs
 and claps her hands.

Easy to store in the memory chunks from *Athalie*
 in that unblasted silence, that jetless sky…
Seventy years on, in Racine's country, when the doctor
 asks about insomnia, she knows why

She hardly suffers it at all. 'What do you do, Madame,
 if you can't sleep?' 'I recite Abner's speech:
Oui, je viens dans son temple adorer l'Éternel; and my eyelids
 filled with sand, close on Judah's beach.'

THE PAINTING

It *was* hers, she'd painted it;
and when exhibited in Paris
with a bowl of rose petals
burning beside it, a sickly-sweet smell
pervaded the air.

'Effective,' said viewers
as they filed past, and whispered,
'Yes, very moving.'

But when I stared into the canvas
it threatened to engulf me –
all that blue, layer upon layer
of thick intellectual blue…
with just a clearing at the bottom
in earth brown

          and below that
her name (as maiden or wife?)
and finally the title:
Une ligne se déplace
pour ceux qui n'ont rien.

PARK BENCH

When I can stand it no longer
I go out and find my bench
overlooking the Seine;
the water's flow quietens me
and the slow barges steady my heart.

The acacia's overhanging branches
protect me like enfolding arms…
I'm safe there.

Little girls in pink dresses
with frilly voices run past,
intent boys on scooters chase them.

I sit trying to read,
but instead I think of you
old lady with steely eyes,
the rigour of a prophet,
a biblical command in your voice;
how sure you are of everything.
But my doubts grow
to the size of the hilltop Sacré-Coeur in the distance
and my anger rises straight, sharp and metallic
like Mr Eiffel's tower opposite.

It's time
to walk back home to you.
You've missed me. Your mood's changed,
mine too. We sit down and eat together.

A DREAM OF HER

Like an Indian princess
adorned for her wedding – gilded,
pomaded, perfumed – she smiles
behind veils, the smile of acceptance.

Jewels hang from her face:
rubies from her lips, from the temples,
diamonds; sapphires and emeralds
from nose and ear lobes.

She goes about
her daily tasks unburdened
by the weight of the stones;
she rinses leaves in clear water

that spills trickling over the tiles,
and the jewels make tiny tinkling tunes
as she moves her head this way
and that, this way and that.

FROM A COLD SPRING

In that apartment facing north
spring was slow to come.
Ill-cut chestnut trees obscured the feeble sun;
we had to walk out to get warm.

I sat opposite you
counting the wrinkles
I hadn't seen before;
some bones protruded further.

Secretly
I fleshed out your cheeks,
pouted your lips, rounded you
into the figure I had known.

Between us
we wove a web of words
that trapped the flying thought
and held it on parched soil.

What does it matter
whether I like Karl Popper,
whether you've read Auden on Kierkegaard
or we both feel a rapport with Lautréamont?

I love you. Isn't that enough?

STRANDED

We sit opposite each other
naming our favourite trees:
yours the oak, mine the cypress.

Outside,
snow settles in a thin line
along the branches

and holds a blackbird
stranded
in a pool of darkness.

A PLEA

Autumn is here; mist
has camouflaged my breath.
Yesterday the wind blew my skirt
right up round my waist.

Behind the lopped chestnut trees
you're still there, nodding to *your* birds.
I see you in the chair facing the window,
with your prayer book in your lap.

Your hands are thin and veined and they fidget.
Now you're looking out beyond the trees,
the clouds, the sky, with a lift of your head
that pulls the sinews in your neck.

Clouds muster towards winter
(Oh let it pass quickly, let it be bearable);
when the spring comes I'll be there with you
and I'll bring you granddaughters, laughter.

EVE OF THE SABBATH

She'll be eating, like every night,
by the sink, in the kitchen, alone.
Though she longs to make the Sabbath special
her brittle legs won't shuttle her
to the living room and back,
with plates and cutlery and food.

So she partly clears the dining table
and lays the embroidered cloth,
folded in half, with two matching napkins,
the tarnished salt-cellar and candlesticks,
and leaves them there till the hour
on Saturday when the sun will set.

MAKING COFFEE

A Snapshot

Spilling is part of it,
signifying plenty, an overflowing.
The thickness of the grind's
perfect for Turkish;
and the sweetness
never cloying. One, two,
three times the liquor
must come to the boil,
then off the flame and rested
till the bubbling froth settles –
startled by a single drop of water –
into recognisable stillness.

You've got your back to us,
but we sense the concentration
in your shoulders and we guess
your smile at the task achieved.

Your head's bowed
into the vapours that rise
from the long-handled pot.

The traditional glass
of cold water sitting
alongside the minuscule cup,
you're reluctant to offer.
Why dilute intense pleasure?

SUMMER'S END

She bends over me,
as if I were a child
lifting my face to hers and waiting
for the bedtime incantation to begin.

Love has struck out time...
yet I see lines, hairs, blemishes,
and behind these her shining hair,
full cheeks, bright eyes.

Outside, a harsher wind
twists the poplar leaves
silver side out. I'm going,
once again I'm waving, waving.

I would go back
but our lives are pulled apart.
I can only go on
to autumn, winter and beyond

to that unimaginable season
of leaflessness
without hope of renewal
without her.

THAT'S HER

That figure in black
bent double in the spring sunshine
disappearing into the dark
under the railway bridge,
that's her…

                  unsteady legs
stockinged in thick brown; in her basket
an old foulard to wrap her bread in; eyes
scanning the pavement for dog mess,
that's her…

                  the socialite, face
behind veils seeded with velvet dots; gloved;
mounted on high heels; snake-skin bag on her arm
and silver fox over her shoulder,
that's her…

                  the socialist
roused by Matteotti; who reads *Le Temps*,
proscribed by Mussolini, and refuses
to hang bunting on the balcony
when Il Duce's motorcade is due to pass,
that's her…

                  she says:
'I'm all right, leave me,
I'm not really alone';
now her eyes brighten: 'I live with God.'

*Giacomo Matteotti: eminent Italian socialist leader assassinated
by the Fascists in 1924.*

BECOMING YOU

Boulogne-sur-mer, August 1993

I telephone you,
I'm here in France.
I'm near you. And I tell you
of my dream – how I cradled you
in my arms and sang…
(I didn't say how light you were).

You tell me of your glass of milk for supper,
your bread and jam for breakfast,
a small piece of chicken for lunch
with two boiled potatoes.

You've told me before,
you tell me again,
and again you give me your blessing:
May the Lord bless you and keep you,
and make His light to shine upon you,
all the days of your life. Amen.
Your voice weakens,
it trails off to a whisper…

     *

Now your light is fading,
your body's slipping into mine,
it will fit there comfortably;
no need to hold it fast.
You're passing into me.
I hear my mouth pronouncing your words.
I hear my breath breathing you.

FIRST-TIME FLIER

When she was very ill
I flew her here
to live with us at home.
She hated it. Her mind
all in a fog, she moaned:
'I'm treated like a dog.'

Each day she'd phone
her neighbour up and say:
'Be there for me, don't go away,
this is not home, I will not stay.
I'm coming back to you.'
So back we flew.

The steward and I
eased her off the chair
and helped her stand
quite steady on her feet
and shuffle down
to her allotted seat.

It was the clouds
impressed her most: 'What clouds!
So many and so close
to God,' she cried.
Then eyed the tea tray
with unhidden greed.

Small English sandwiches
were not for her,
but scones to dip
uncut into her drink
and jam to spoon
out of the jar and lick.

This first-time flier
flew at eighty-nine.
On take-off, she slipped
her thin hand in mine:
'This is no plane,
it's a train... in the clouds.'

STATUETTE

The Royal Doulton little girl
in her long white nightie,
head to one side supported
by a chubby hand under the chin,
standing demurely to say good night,
her tidy blond hair in a halo, was me.
You said so.

She's not me now.
I'm not innocent, nor small,
nor golden-haired, nor kind to you,
now you're old and eat
with the hunger of a beast,
and sleep with your cheeks sucked in,
your eyebrows knitted into anger
and your fingers curled like claws.

How can I reach you?
Now words, our long-time friends
and bearers of exquisite messages,
no longer bridge us; when you read
and cannot register. And I, impatient,
voice the same passage over and over,
angry at your snail's pace,
your failure to understand.

Statuette in the flowing nightie,
teach me to be kind
and play the grown-up game,
be mother to this child,
and come, not needing to know why,
like a mother to her baby's cry.

COMFORTERS

She rolled her hankies into little mice
(the way she did for me when I was small)
with tail and ears, and laid them out in rows;
at night they nestled into bed with her.

I seldom saw her blow her nose in one –
she just liked having them around, to hand,
in apron pocket or tucked in her sleeve –
and should she lose one, it was, 'On your knees.'

The day she died I gathered up the mice,
(I didn't dare dispose of them too soon)
arranged them round her body on the floor
to give her comfort as they'd done before.

SKY

You would have loved the sky the day we buried you,
Of deep then deeper blue like on your island home,
The thinning poplars, planes shedding their mustard leaves.

There were no flowers – you hated cutting them –
But from your long-lost home a piece of rue
Thrown on the coffin lid beside your name.

The rabbi too, the sort you would have liked: modest
In manner, crumpled suit, scuffed shoes, intoned the prayer
Basso profundo, with no sense of pressing time.

A few wore black, others, vivid colours; and some
Sobbed quietly, but no ululation or despair.
All-round acceptance in that clear and weightless air

Of things that are and were and pass beyond
The limits of our bounded life. I heard your voice
Say: leave me now, I'm perfectly at peace.

And still I come to tell you this… you who hated
Funerals, never spoke of them nor went to any.

HER HAIR

She always did her hair up in a bun.
Once in her life she strayed and had a perm.
It wasn't her; she let it all grow out.

I never knew her frizzed. For me
her hair was furrow-straight; cat-black and bright
almost to the end. At night, uncoiled,

it hung about her shoulders like a girl's
(she'd worn it in an ample plait at school)
and gave her strong-lined face a gentler look.

The last time, on the floor, her hair was limp.
I thought to cut some off… decided not,
and didn't even keep her pearly combs,

her pins like tuning forks in tortoise-shell
(the smaller ones she'd lose at every turn
and bid all those around her look for them).

LAST FITTING

'She's too tiny,' said the men,
'we don't do a smaller one,
the next size down's a child's.'

She'd shrunk, living alone
and eating when she remembered.
They asked for a cushion;

I gave them the big stiff one
we called sergeant-major
with the urn patterns on the chintz.

(It bolstered her up
when she gave us her bed
and curled up on the settee

like a foetus, saying she felt
no need to stretch out
and that she'd sleep like a top…)

They tucked it in at her feet
to keep her from sliding
when they carried her down the stairs.

Now we're saying prayers around
the tasselled cover with the silver Star,
and the two long-time neighbours

from across the landing
whisper to each other: 'tu vois,
elle était Protestante.'

It's time to carry her out.
I hear a childish voice – though not a child's –
screaming NO, NO,

you can't take her,
you're not allowed,
you can't take my mother.

SORTING THINGS OUT

A wooden spoon.
A sieve. That special saucepan for the rice.
A toothpick-holder made of glass
(it travelled with us from Milan).
A bunch of porcelain flowers in fashion then.

Your father's letters
in that odd Ladino/Hebrew mix
(Ladino sound with Hebrew script).
Your brother's, when his wartime marriage failed;
the paper blotchy, dampened, then dried up.

Your clothes: the suit you did your teaching in;
the 'White House' blouses I'd bring from London;
the silver fox whose muzzle bit its tail-end with a grin.
The moiré dress and jacket, bluey-grey,
the seamstress made you for my wedding day.

I haven't kept all these.
I've given them away.
I'm tired of keepsakes.

Your voice I'm keeping though,
your ringing Gallic voice close to my ear;
the rough feel of your hand scrubbing my back
the thick ring on your finger hurting me.

PICKFORDS

Sharp at eight, they were there
to pack it all: views of the Alps,
the wedding group where no one smiles
and everyone's in black (save bride and maids).
Theodor Herzl inventing the future from the rail
of a hotel balcony in Basle.

The old Philips in two-tone walnut
with Alvar Lidell's voice still inside.

The brass pestle and mortar
she would squat at, determined
to pound everything to crumbs.
Two ears of wheat she'd smuggled
into Africa to remind her of Europe.

The scroll of the Book of Esther
encased in a silver tube.
His prayer books in Hebrew only;
hers in Hebrew and French.
My book of Pinocchio, his nose on the cover
shortened by age, but legs still striding.

Deftly they made trestle tables
and laid everything out
so you could see each object clearly
at angles you never saw before;
the blemishes even, the film of dust on them,
and touch them if you wanted to.

They cut and shaped
pieces of cardboard into boxes
lined with newspaper and polystyrene;
and they wrapped the more fragile things
in white tissue like shrouds. Each box
fastened and sealed with strong, sticky strips.

When they'd finished
all you saw was boxes.

ON NOT FOLLOWING INSTRUCTIONS

1

'Bury her Bible with her,' the aunt ordered.
Would my mother go on reading in the tomb?
Would it impress her Maker more
when they came face to face?
Would the worms go for that first?

I know the ancient Egyptians did it:
food (leg of lamb), drinking vessels,
bronze mirrors, jewellery and trinkets,
and games to while away the hours
on the long journey to Eternity.

But my mother? She didn't even take
her bedtime book – *Don Quixote* –
when she went for her femur operation.
'I want to think,' she said, 'and sleep.'

2

'Your mother's grave is overgrown,
You really should attend to it;
Right now we barely see the stone.'

But mother loved wild flowers and weeds,
Loathed cutting things to put in pots:
'Do we cut off children's heads?' she'd plead.

Re dirt and dust, she used to say:
'Both dirt and dust will still be there,
Long after we have gone away.'

Better the gentle rubbing of a plant –
What harm can dandelions do? –
Than your determined scrubbing-brush, dear aunt.

REGRET

That I wasn't with you when you died,
Nor heard it when you cried

Falling from your bed;
Nor placed a pillow there beneath your head.

Not to have loosened up your clothes for air,
Nor straightened out your tangled hair.

Not to have said your last *Shema* with you
Who'd taught me it when words were new.

Not to have shut your staring eyes
Nor closed your open mouth; its unheard cries.

And covered your small body;
And covered you as well

With such prayers as I know
That mean fare well.

COMBAT

Since you died
mine's a posthumous life.

I capture your voice
by talking to myself in French
and scanning your library –
your favourite authors: Molière, Racine,
Valéry, Supervielle, Yourcenar…
I long to discuss them with you,
to lock horns in deadly combat –
two rivals unwittingly
searching out the same prize.

It was sweet torture,
your indifferent response
to my 'Mum, I'm coming over
to stay with you for a few weeks.'
– Yes, you do as you like –
Was this what you really meant?

Correct me, scold me,
reprimand, chastise me,
but *be* there –
not this black hole
imploding, collapsing further
each day.

Were you here now,
you'd tell me again I'm wrong,
wrong not to let go,
wrong to grieve so,
ferociously.

TRIOLETS

Psalm

Is she still there
Reading a psalm
In her chintz-covered chair?
I know she's not there
Inhaling the air
Of the room's rich calm.
Yet I still see her there
Reading her psalm.

The Intercom

There's a click-clack of heels on the parquet floor
When she hears the intercom bell
And runs to open the door.
Now her heels on the parquet floor
Tap a muted ghostly encore
Repeating as if in a spell
That click-clack of heels on the parquet floor
When she hears the intercom bell.

The Balcony

Is she still there
On the balcony, waving,
Whispering a prayer?
I know she's not there
And the balcony's bare –
She can't bless our leaving.
Yet I still see her there
On the balcony, waving.

VOICE

I hear your voice that last time on the phone
(By then a shaky voice but strong inside)
Whenever I feel scared or too alone
And I'm indifferent if it praise or chide.

You solemnly, in lower pitch, intone
The words that nourished you, time-honoured, tried.
They helped you feel at ease in the unknown,
When countryless, these prayers became your guide.

You say *shalom, shalom, shalom*. You've grown
To love the word as you prepare to glide
Into the silent world where bone and stone
Are one; fear would be undignified.

I dial, the receiver's at my ear;
Your voice is now both distant and so near.

COUNTRY LANE IN CORNWALL

In my ears, the wind;
in my sight, the sea.
But your voice rises,
rises from inside me,
and deafens the wind,
and drowns the sea.

JUST ASKING

'If you speak to the dead, you bring them back to life.'
Egyptian saying

How is it there,
Now time has passed,
At the end of the row
In a plot by the wall –
Like a corner table
At *Le Parnassien* café,
Away from the crowd?

Is it still cosy
In the satin-lined box,
Your head on a small
Lace-edged pillow – like
The one you brought with you
On your trips to see us?

Are you resting your femur,
Your spine, prolapsed womb,
Conversing with sparrows,
Praising their churr,
Testing the timeless,
Losing your selfdom,
Fleeing the tomb?

BALLADESQUE

The song 'Paris c'est une blonde', a favourite of my
mother's, was popular in the 1920s and 1930s.

Is it wrong to want to forget
That August in Paris with you?
Our pleasure uncaging that pet
To let it go sing in the blue.
Blonde Paris was empty once more;
The trees and the plants had their reign,
And fragrances swam at the door,
Remembering comes laden with pain.

The aunt who'd fidget and fret,
Too often laid low with the 'flu,
But promptly would rise to collect
Us at the *Nord*, hat all askew.
Can one put things back as before?
So many 'clips' crowd the brain
In memory's overfull store,
Remembering comes laden with pain.

There's Pierre Balmain's seamstress, your friend,
Who, kneeling, begged you to stay
When she saw your friendship may end
With my plan to take you away.
Sharp-eyed, petite, very French,
She taught me a risqué refrain
We'd sing on our shady park bench.
Remembering comes laden with pain.

The last time I photographed you
(Wish the camera'd lied once again)
Flesh had gone; skull only came through.
Remembering comes laden with pain.

TOGETHER IN MONTPARNASSE

'Les morts cachés sont bien dans cette terre.'
Paul Valéry, *Le Cimitière Marin*

They were none of them your friends,
yet they were more than friends,
they could do no wrong; your artists,
poets, musicians, thinkers.

You'd forgive them their misdemeanours,
callousness, self-conceit, because
they were 'different, higher,
far removed from the common herd.'

They were your 'great men' (seldom women)
and here they all are, levelled, same,
rubbing shoulder-blades in death's
comprehensive list.

See in the Sixth Division Section Two
is Charles Baudelaire who urged us
to remember his childhood maidservant,
'qui dort son sommeil sous une humble pelouse.'

Not far from him is Jean Sablon whose *fiacre*
you loved to hear trotting by. Between them
lies the king of the absurd, now
fully vindicated: Eugène Ionesco.

Exceptionally Sartre and Simone de Beauvoir
you couldn't stand; and you disdained
Marguerite Duras' bestsellers. They're in the Twentieth,
she in the Twenty-first Division.

Diagonally across from you is Sainte-Beuve
for whom literature was a religion
ardemment embrassée dès l'enfance,
as it was for you.

And young Robert Desnos is here
who howled, *Je n'aime plus la rue Saint-Martin,*
when his friend was taken away one morning.
He was brought back dead from Terezin

and interred in the Fifteenth Division
between Bourdelle and Chaim Soutine whose
anguish brushed his carcasses with blood,
prophetic of the human abattoirs to come.

In the Twenty-eighth Division is Captain Dreyfus,
traduced and vilified, back from Devil's Island
an ill and broken man; now lying to attention
under the heavy, worm-eaten Tricolour.

Two Divisions down you can look up Pierre Larousse,
his weighty dictionary open at *Les Planches des Beaux Arts.*
(I see you point to Ingres' *Le Bain Turc,*
your eyes wet for your Turkish childhood.)

'Not I, Not I,' shouts Samuel Beckett
in the Twelfth, as if that mouth
opening and shutting endlessly on a Babel of words
could stave off anything… in the end was the Word.

When the winter winds blow over you,
I pray they bring you the haunting tune
from César Franck's *Prélude, Chorale et Fugue.*
Perfect in a mist. He's in the Twenty-sixth.

Music too from Camille Saint-Saëns in the Thirteenth.
He'll play you his *Carnival of the Animals* in which
the swan dies so gracefully and is never, ever buried,
And your favourite arias from *Samson and Delilah.*

And you, my mother, there, in your corner by the gate
(for a quick getaway should Resurrection come?)
away from the throng, your name and dates,
as requested, incised on a simple marble stele:

SARAH SIMSON 1903–1994

THE ISLAND

They waved and they smiled,
my mother, my husband;
on their small rocky island
they stood looking out.

My boat passed by leisurely,
there was no landing jetty
and I wouldn't have stopped
and they didn't want it.

Only smiling and waving
they watched me go by.
There was no calling back
no sound in their voices.

And I woke full of joy
for their calm on their island,
while my boat sailed on
through the reeds and the marshes.

Dalyan, Southern Anatolia, August 1998